HOW DO HUMANS BREATHE?

Science Book Age 8
Children's Biology Books

BABY PROFESSOR

EDUCATION KIDS

Speedy Publishing LLC

40 E. Main St. #1156

Newark, DE 19711

www.speedypublishing.com

Copyright 2017

In this book, we're going to explain how humans breathe. So, let's get right to it!

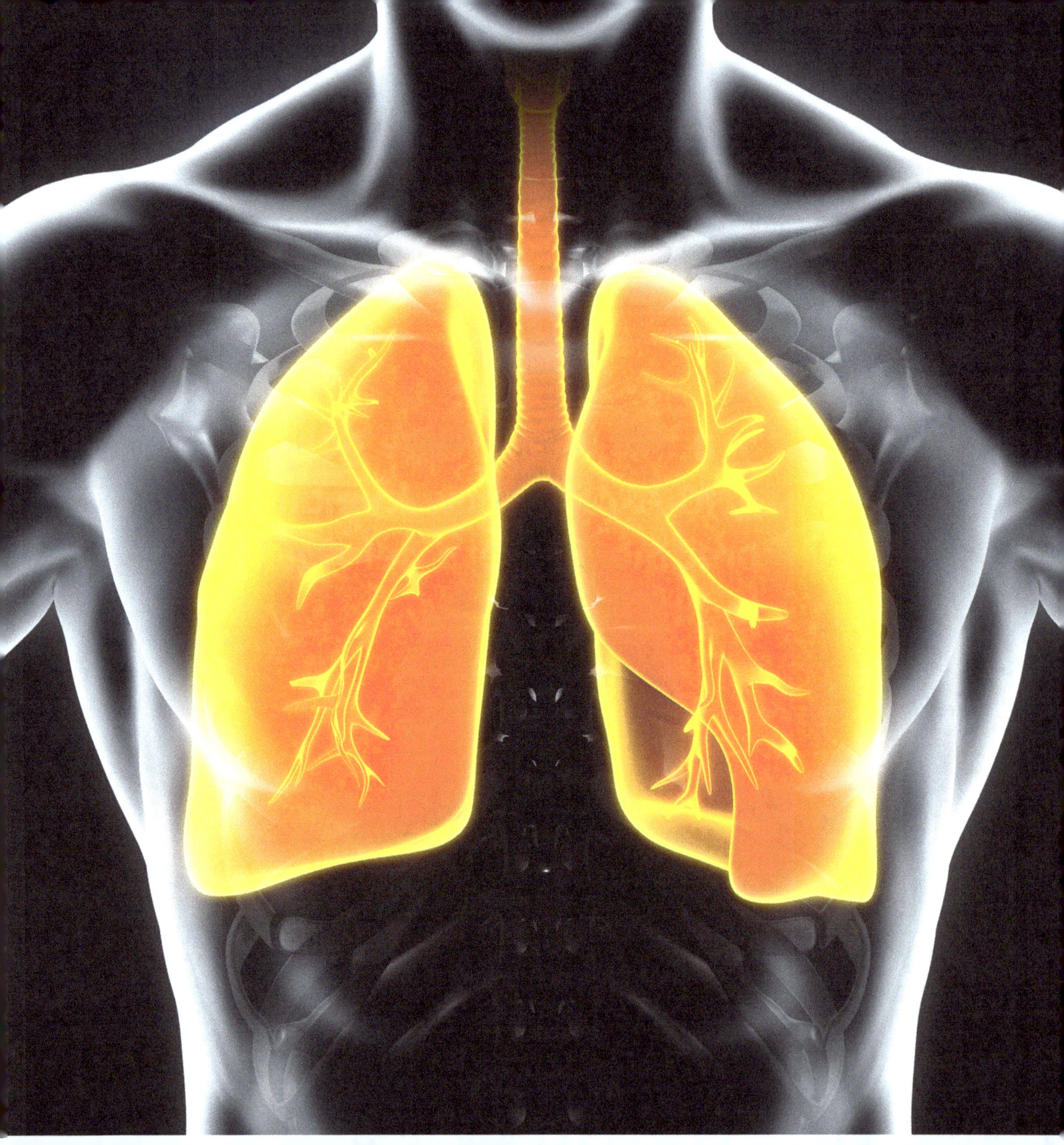

THE RESPIRATORY SYSTEM

The system in your body that is responsible for you getting the oxygen you need to live is called the respiratory system. All of the tissues as well as the organs in your body that allow you to breathe are part of this system.

This system consists of your airways, your two lungs, and all the vessels that carry blood throughout the system. There are also muscles in your diaphragm and abdomen that help you to pull the air in and expel it out. The respiratory system brings oxygen to every part of your body. As you breathe the oxygen-filled air, you exhale a waste gas called carbon dioxide.

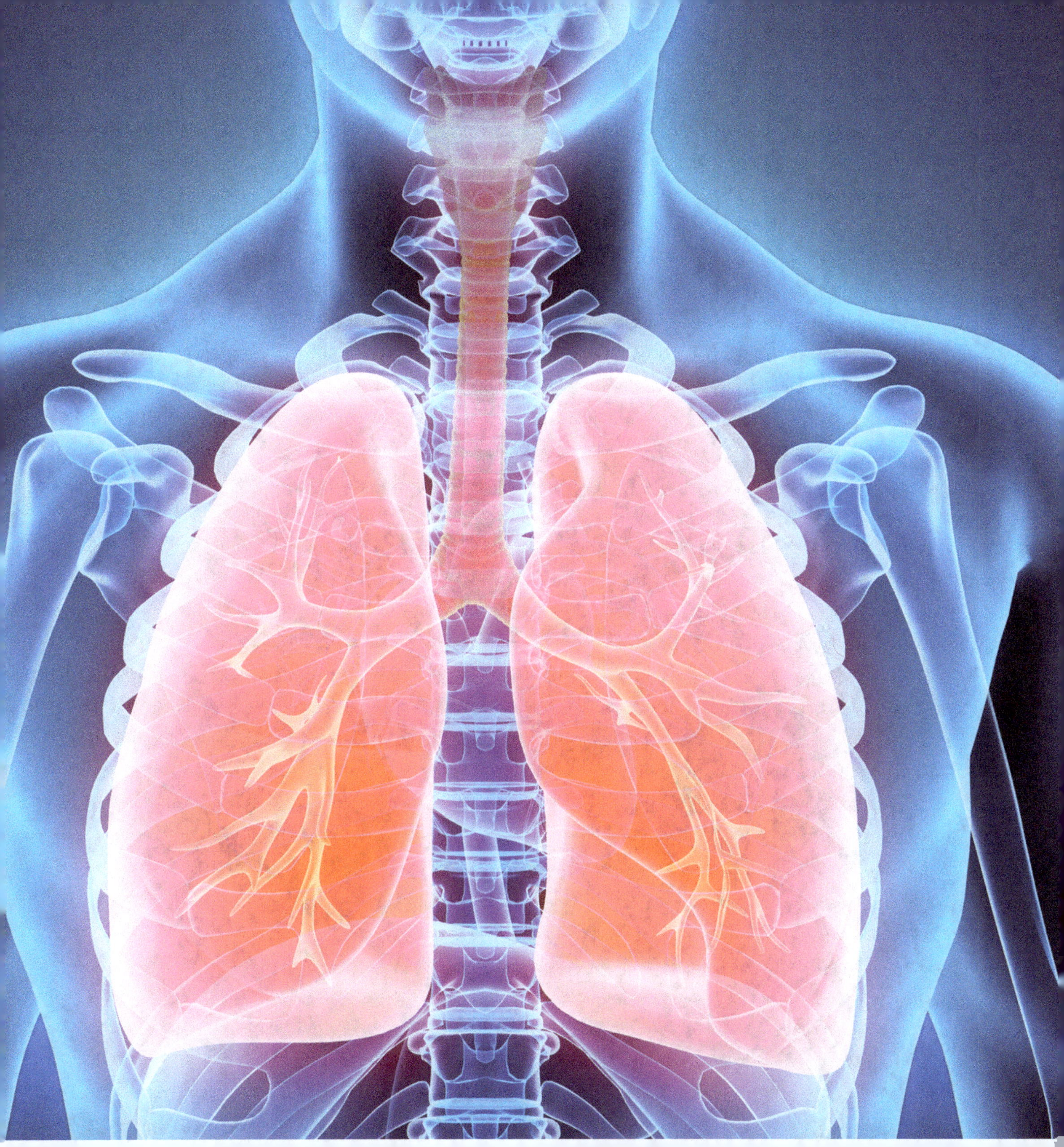

YOUR FIRST BREATH

Before you are born, you're inside your mother's womb and there's no air in there. Your lungs are filled with fluid. During the first few breaths of life, there's still fluid in your lungs that has to be removed through your blood as well as your lymph system.

The very first few breaths you take are some of the most difficult you'll take until your tiny lungs get used to filling up with oxygen. Your lungs have to begin to breathe in oxygen and let out carbon dioxide. Also, blood starts circulating rapidly in your lungs.

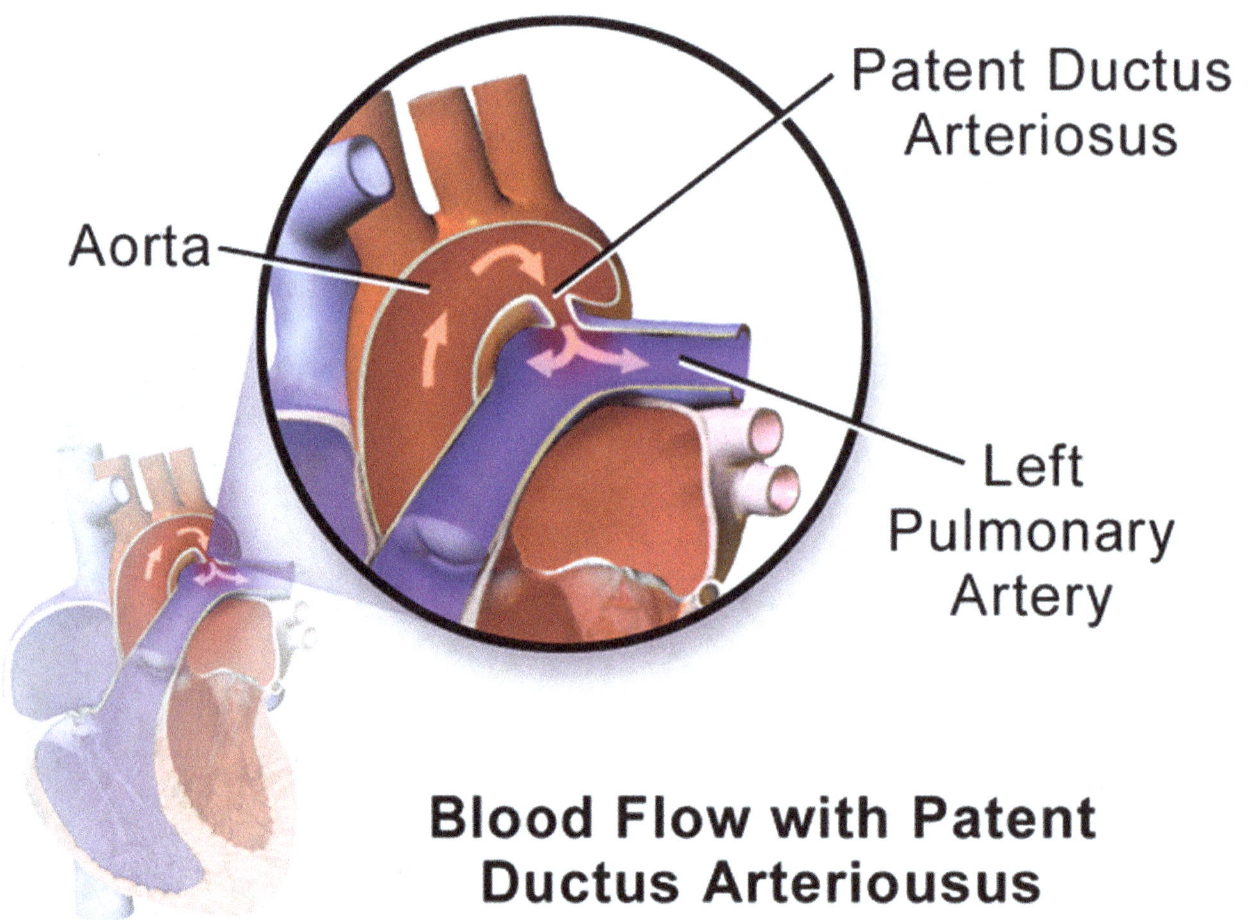

Blood Flow with Patent Ductus Arteriousus

The increasing oxygen causes a blood vessel called the **ductus arteriosus** to begin sealing up. Before birth, this blood vessel was important because it channeled blood away from the lungs, but now you need blood for your lungs to work. After the first or second day of life, the ductus arteriosus isn't needed any longer so it closes up.

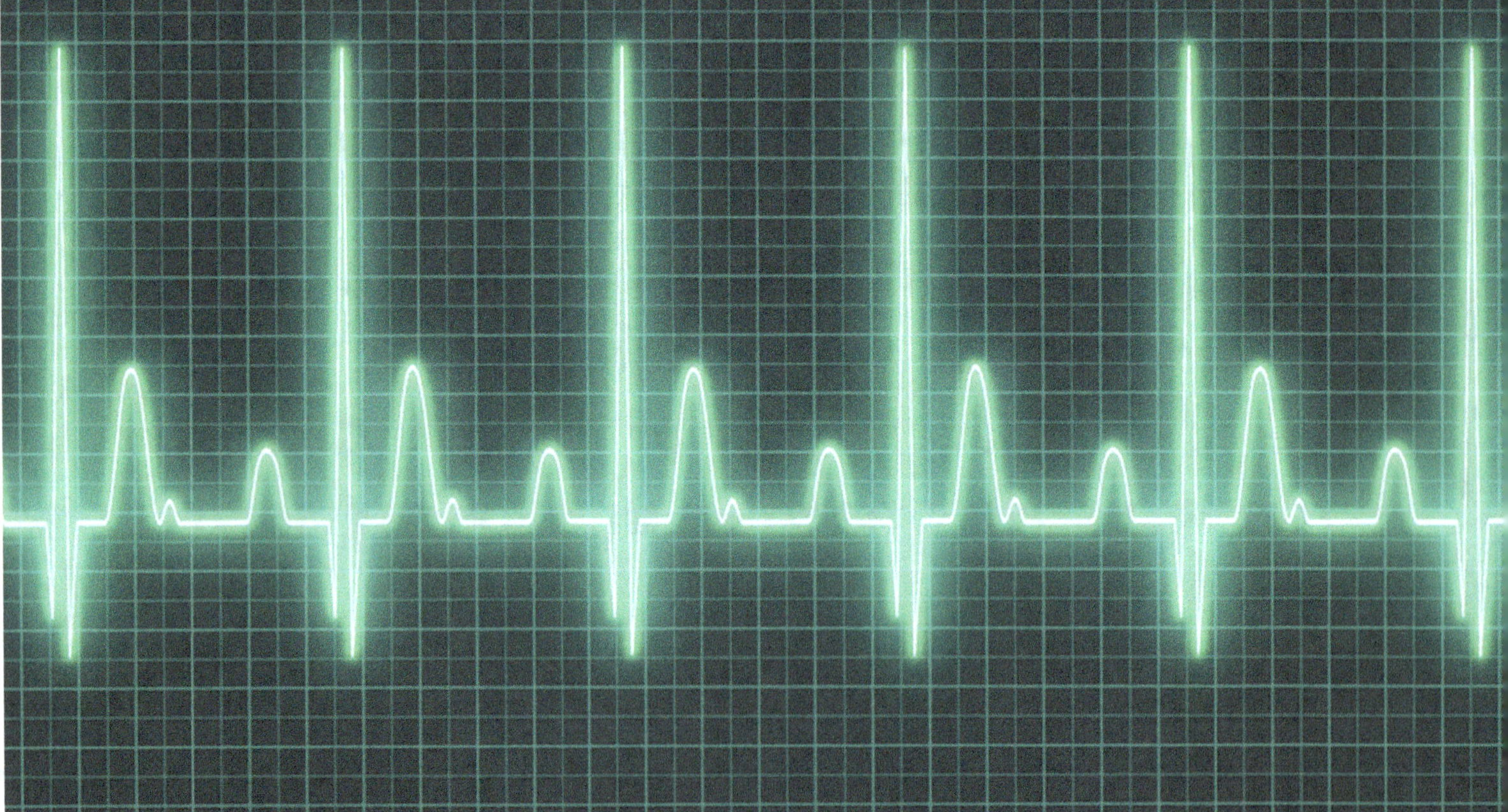

For the rest of your life, until you take your very last breath before you die, you'll take about 15-25 breaths a minute. Most of the time, you won't even be conscious of your breathing, although if you stop and think about it, you can control your breathing to go slower or faster.

A JOURNEY TO THE LUNGS

When you breathe you take in air through your nose or your mouth or both. This wets the air and also warms it. The air you breathe in is only about 20% oxygen and you exhale about 15% oxygen. You breathe in about 11,000 liters of air daily so it's a lot of work for your muscles and lungs, but only about 550 liters of it is the pure oxygen you need to survive.

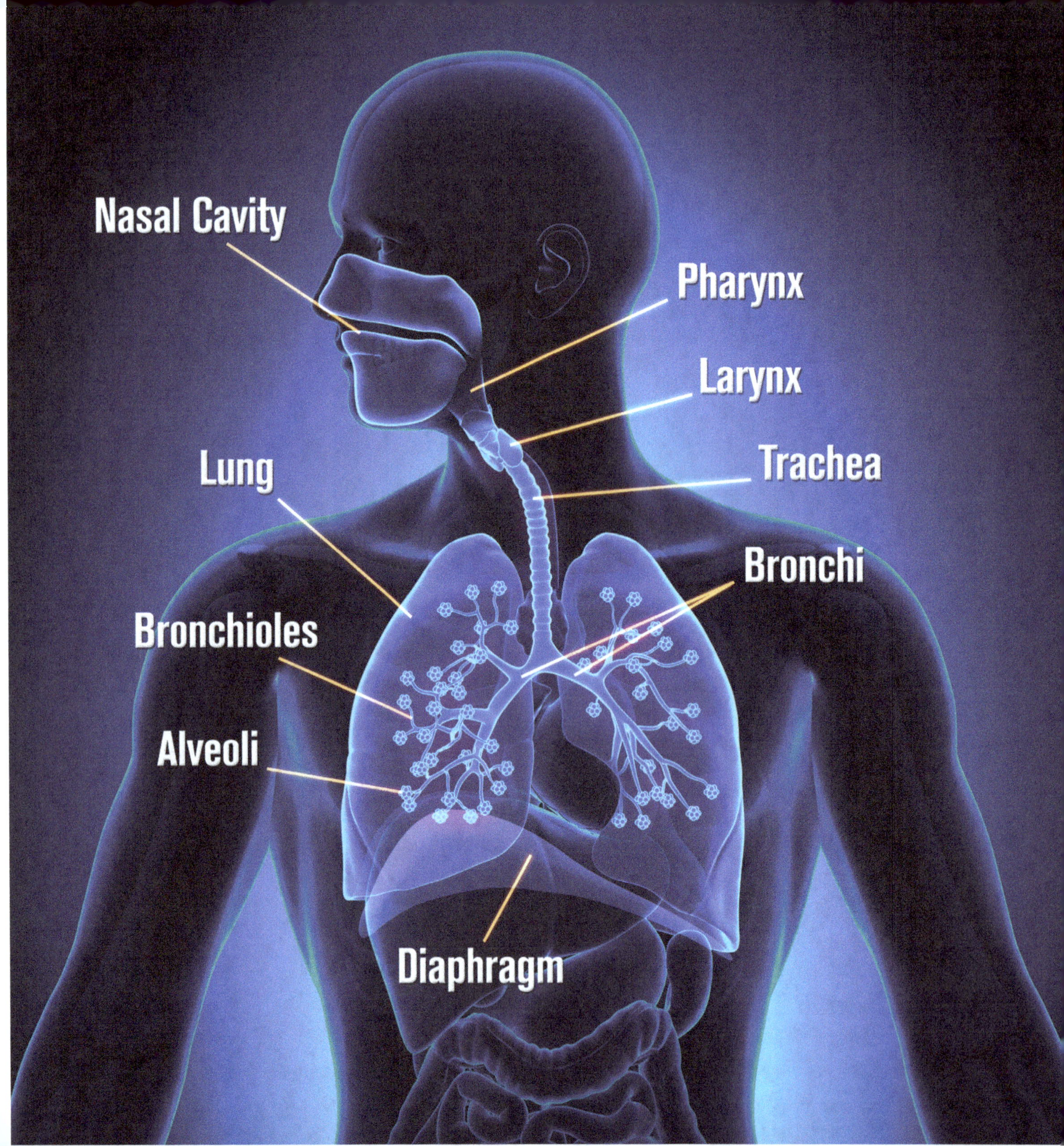

Nasal Cavity
Pharynx
Larynx
Trachea
Lung
Bronchi
Bronchioles
Alveoli
Diaphragm

As you inhale, the air journeys down your throat into your trachea, which is also called your windpipe. There is a tiny flap of tissue here called the epiglottis that shields your windpipe when you swallow. If you're eating and you start to cough, it means that a particle of food went down "the wrong pipe."

As the air continues to be pulled in, the passage divides into two passages. One passage goes to each lung. These passages are the bronchial tubes. In order for your breathing to be free and clear, these tubes need to be free from swelling or mucus.

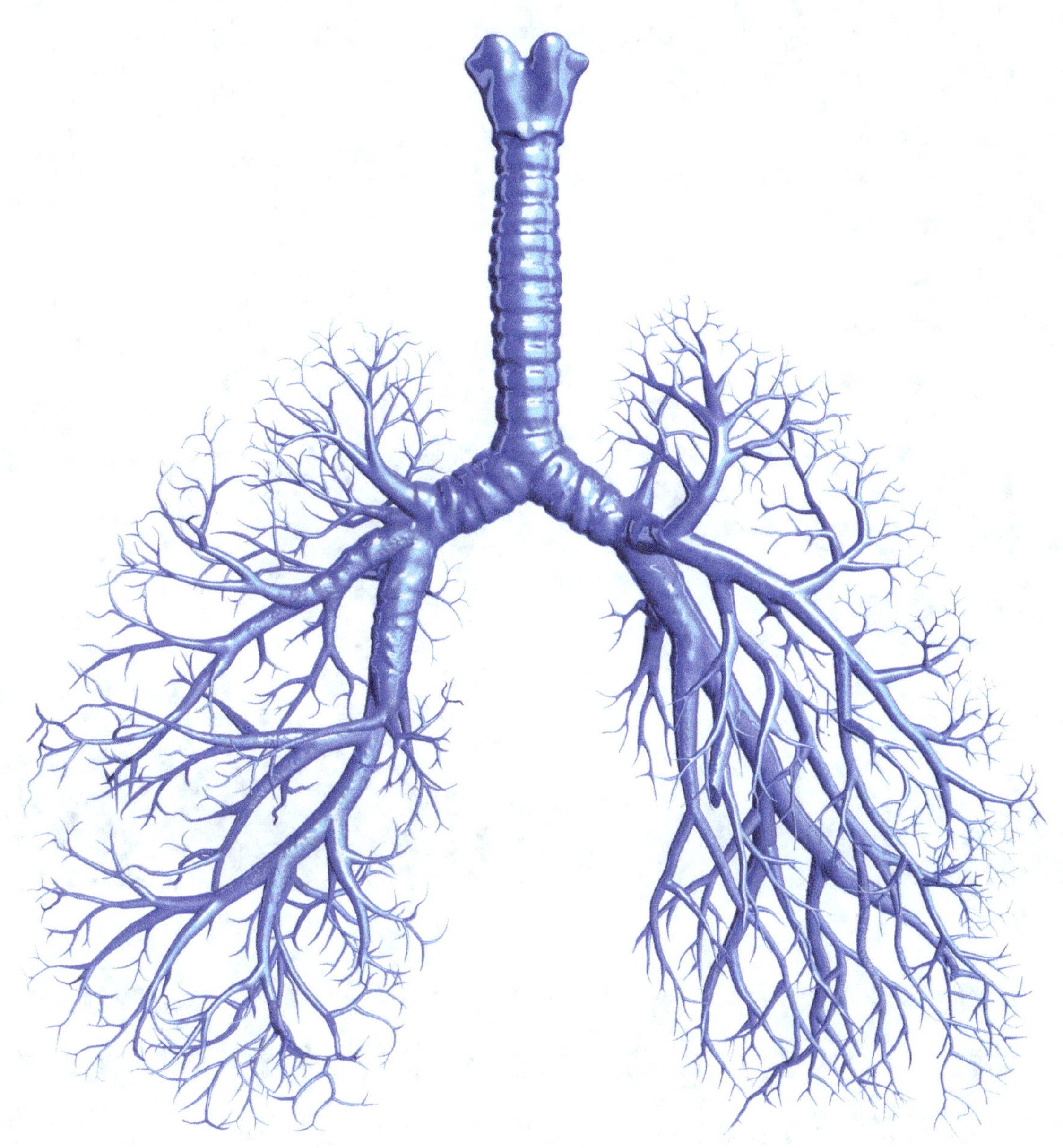

Bronchial tubes

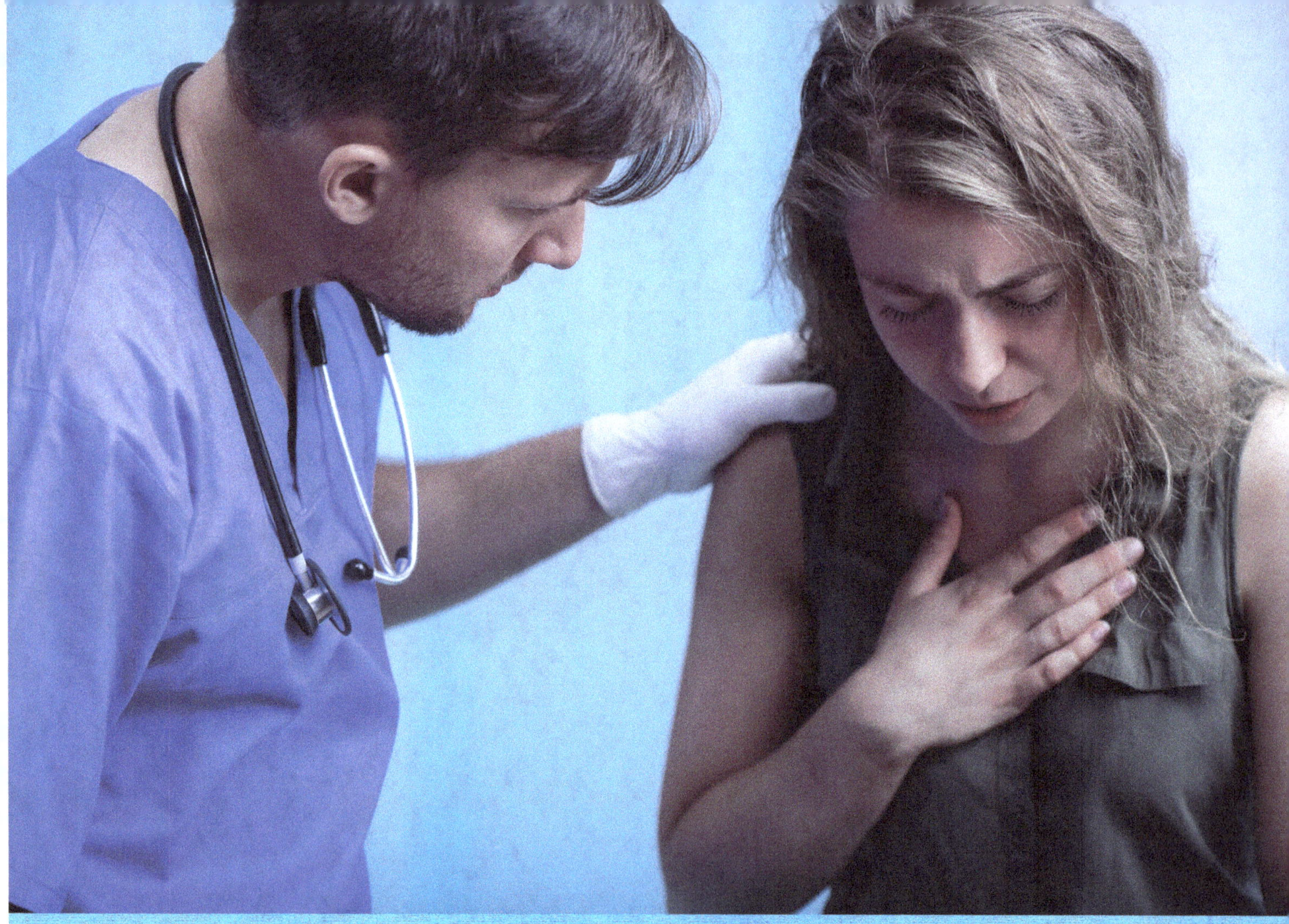

That is why if you have the flu and develop bronchitis, it becomes difficult to breathe. Your bronchial tubes are inflamed and sometimes filled with mucus. More than 3 million people a year in the US suffer from bronchitis.

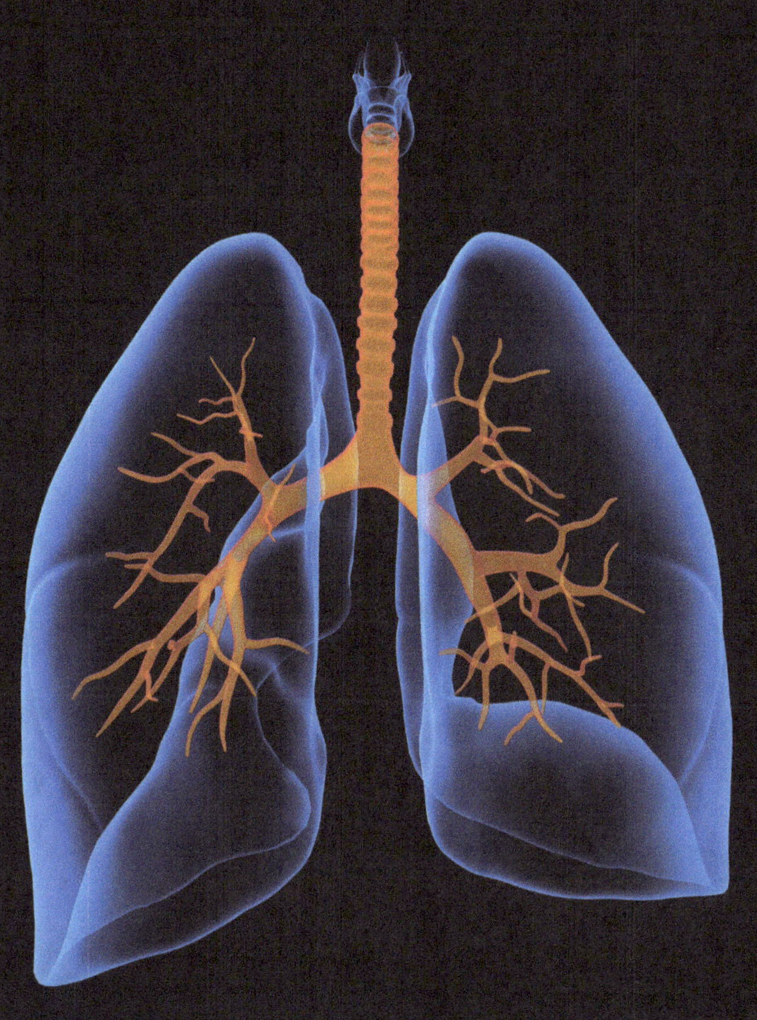

As your bronchial tubes go into the lungs they branch out into smaller and smaller air passages. These passages are called bronchioles and they end in tiny air sacs. These tiny air sacs fill up and deflate just like balloons.

They are called **alveoli**. Your body has as many as 300 million of these alveoli. The alveoli are made of a special thin tissue, which is called squamous epithelial tissue. In addition to being very thin, this tissue is very elastic. The alveoli sacs make the lungs look like sponges.

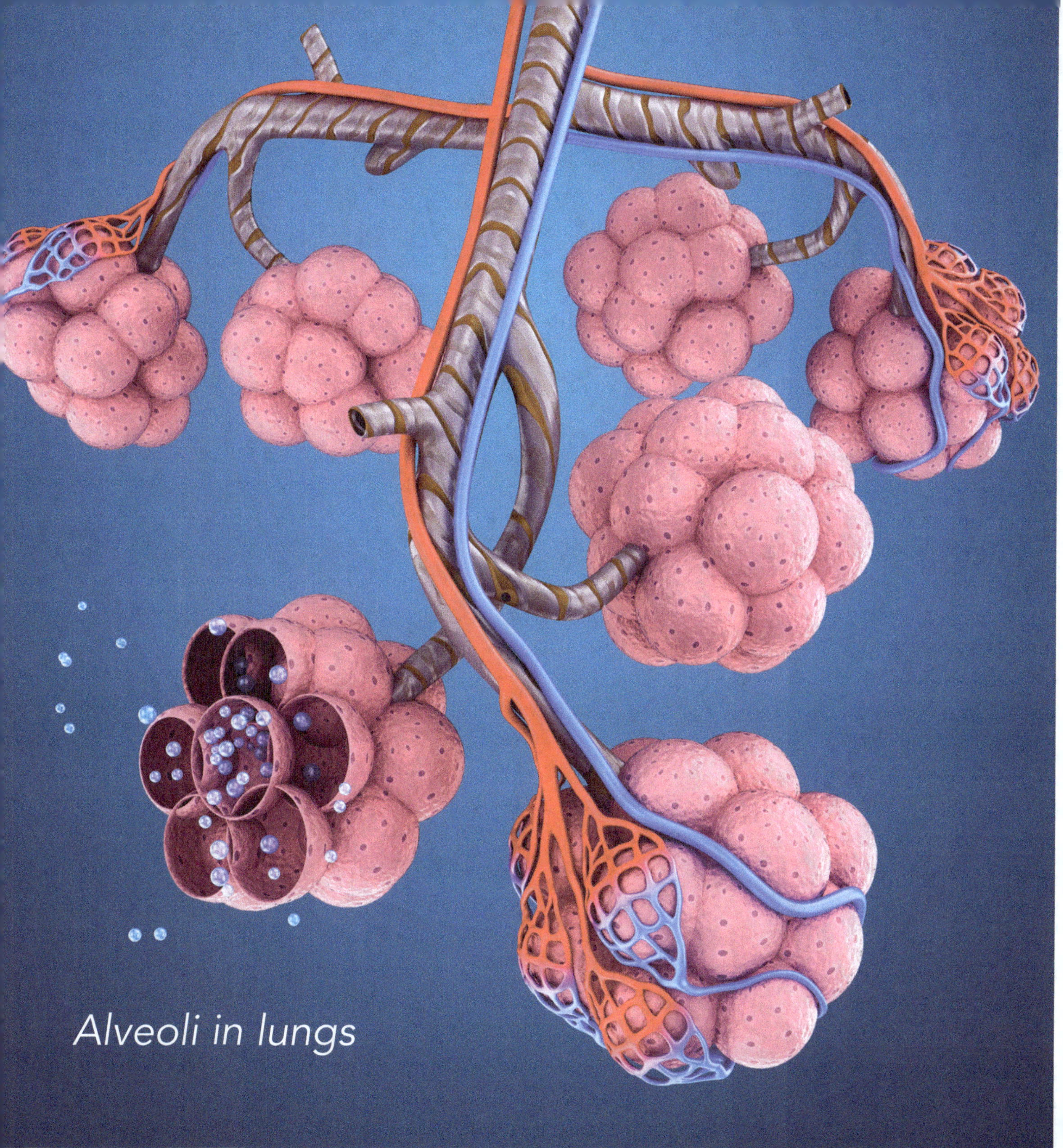

Alveoli in lungs

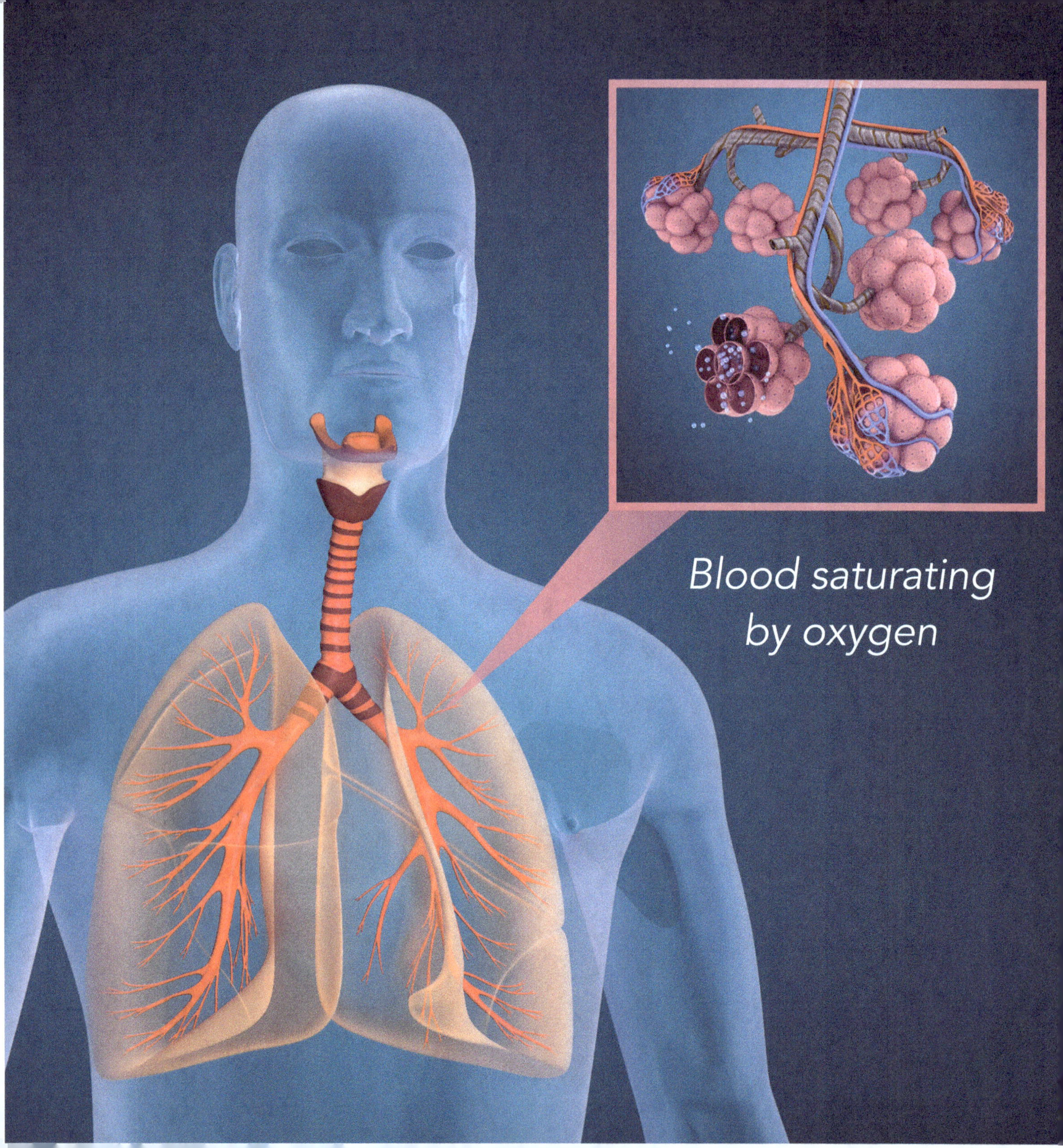

Blood saturating
by oxygen

HOW DOES OXYGEN GET TO THE BLOOD?

Each of the bronchiole gives air to a group of alveoli. These clusters are called alveoli sacs. Each sac is encircled by a bed of capillaries, which is a web of tiny blood vessels. The walls of these blood vessels, and the inflating and deflating thin walls of the alveoli are incredibly thin.

This makes it possible for an exchange to happen. The molecules of oxygen pass from the pumped-up alveoli to special blood cells that carry red blood inside the blood vessels. Then, the molecules of carbon dioxide go from the red blood cells into the alveoli and the carbon dioxide is exhaled out of the lungs. This is how oxygen gets from the respiratory system to the circulatory system.

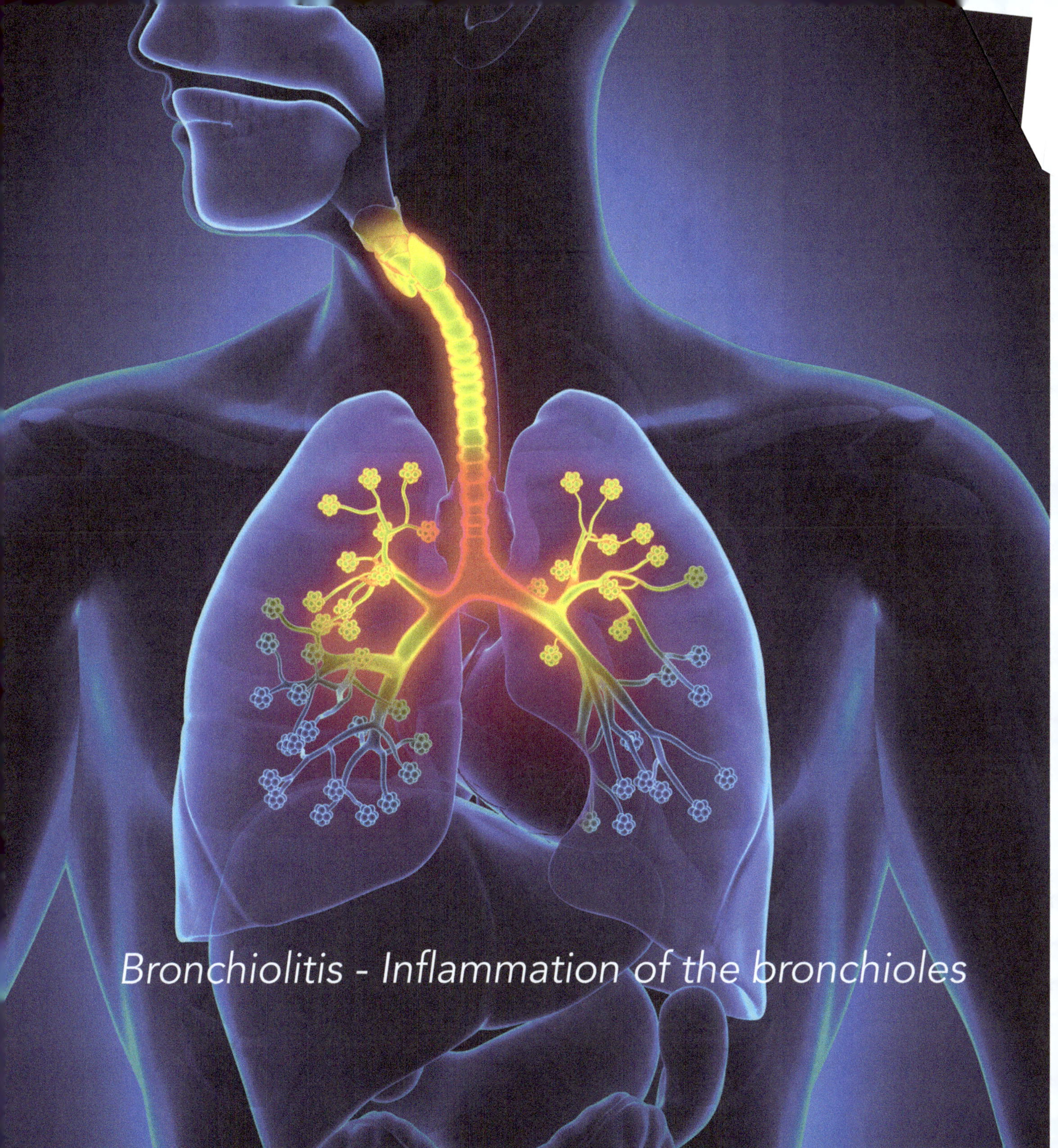

Bronchiolitis - Inflammation of the bronchioles

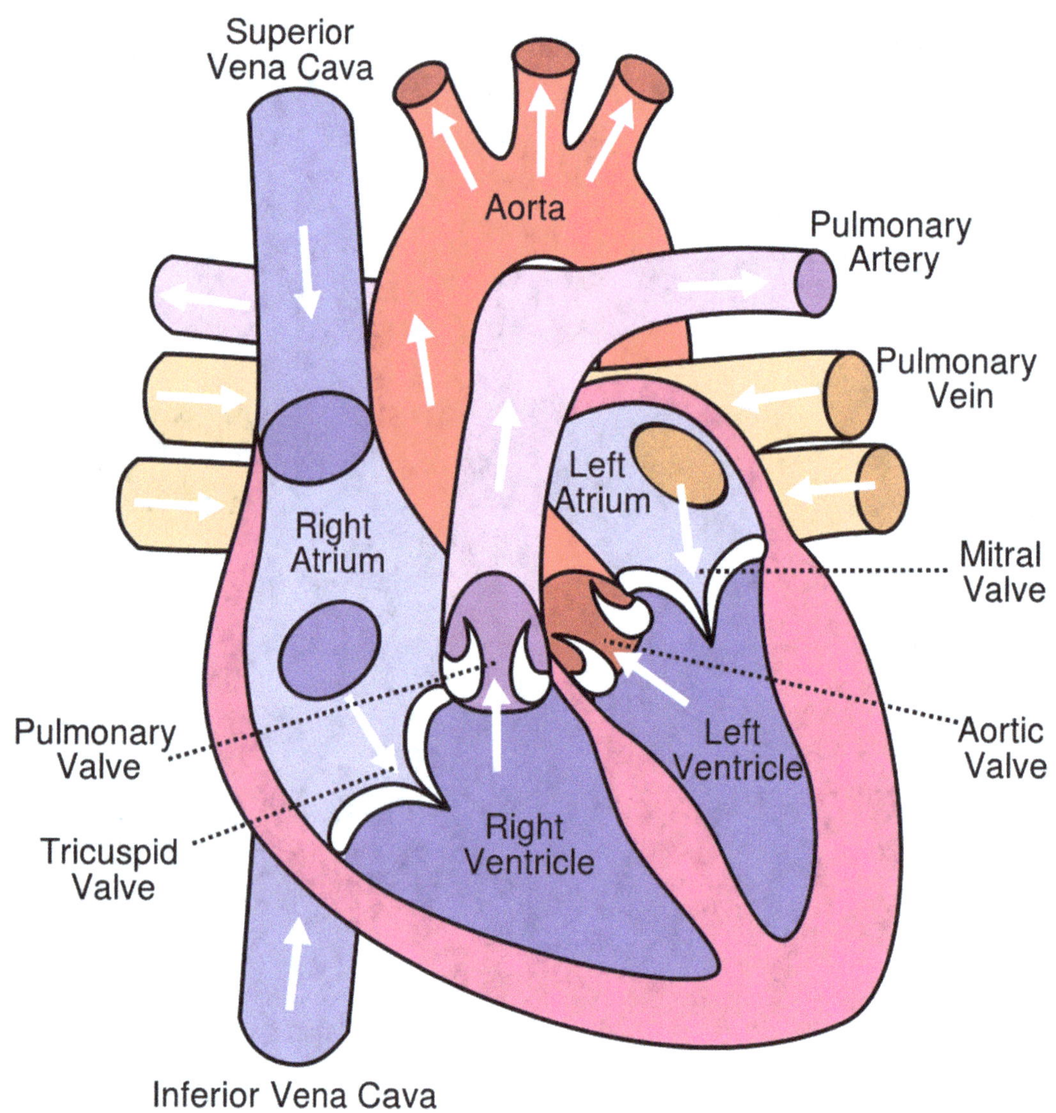

The Human Heart

Fortified with oxygen, the blood is carried from capillaries to the pulmonary vein, which brings blood to the heart's left side. Then, that side of the heart begins to pump the oxygen-rich blood throughout the body.

Every cell inside your body needs oxygen to stay alive. Oxygen is needed to provide the breakdown of simple sugar, also called glucose, so that your cells have the energy to perform their specialized tasks. If carbon dioxide didn't leave your body, eventually it would be toxic to your cells.

*Senior woman at home with portable
oxygen tank*

FILTERING THE AIR

Your respiratory system has ways of keeping out substances that could be harmful to your lungs. There are hairs in your nose that prevent large particles such as grains of pepper or dirt from going down your air passages. Thousands of

microscopic hairs, which are called cilia, line the insides of air passages.

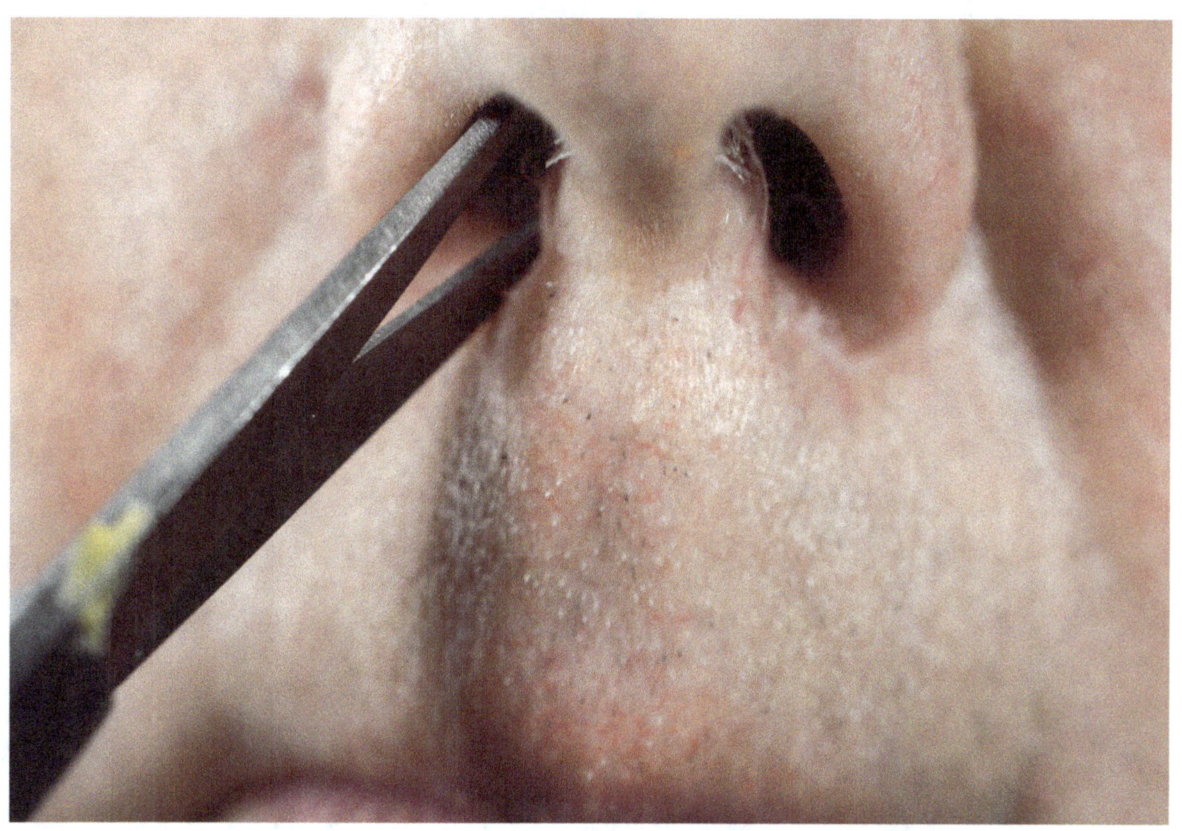

The hairs in a nose are a natural air filter.

Cough

They move in unison in a sweeping motion to help keep the air passages free and clear. Some substances, like cigarette smoke, can cause these cilia to stop working correctly and can bring on bronchitis or other more serious lung diseases.

When we think of mucus we often think of the excess mucus we have when we're sick with a cold or flu. However, some mucus in the trachea and the two bronchial tubes is vital because it keeps out fine dust, viruses, and bacteria as well as substances that cause allergic reactions.

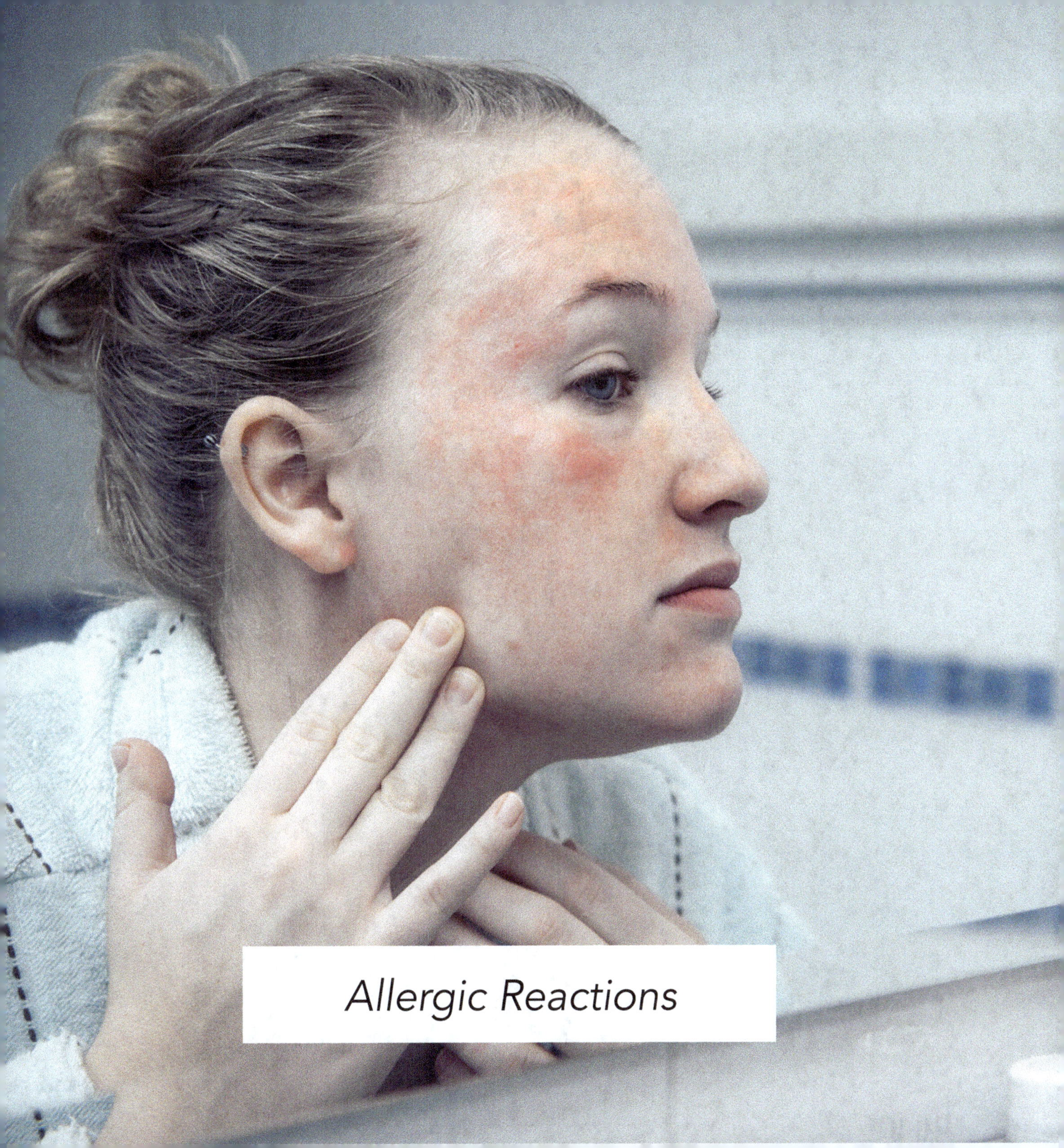

Allergic Reactions

Despite the efforts of our bodies to prevent this from happening, sometimes impurities do get into the deeper parts of the lungs. They can often be coughed up or swallowed or moved out of the body in excess mucous.

WHAT MAKES THE AIR GO IN AND OUT?

The **pleural cavity** is formed by your ribs, which are sets of curved bones, and your diaphragm. The **diaphragm** is a dome-shaped, thick muscle like a horizontal sheet that separates the lungs and heart from the abdominal organs. It's attached to the bottom of the ribs.

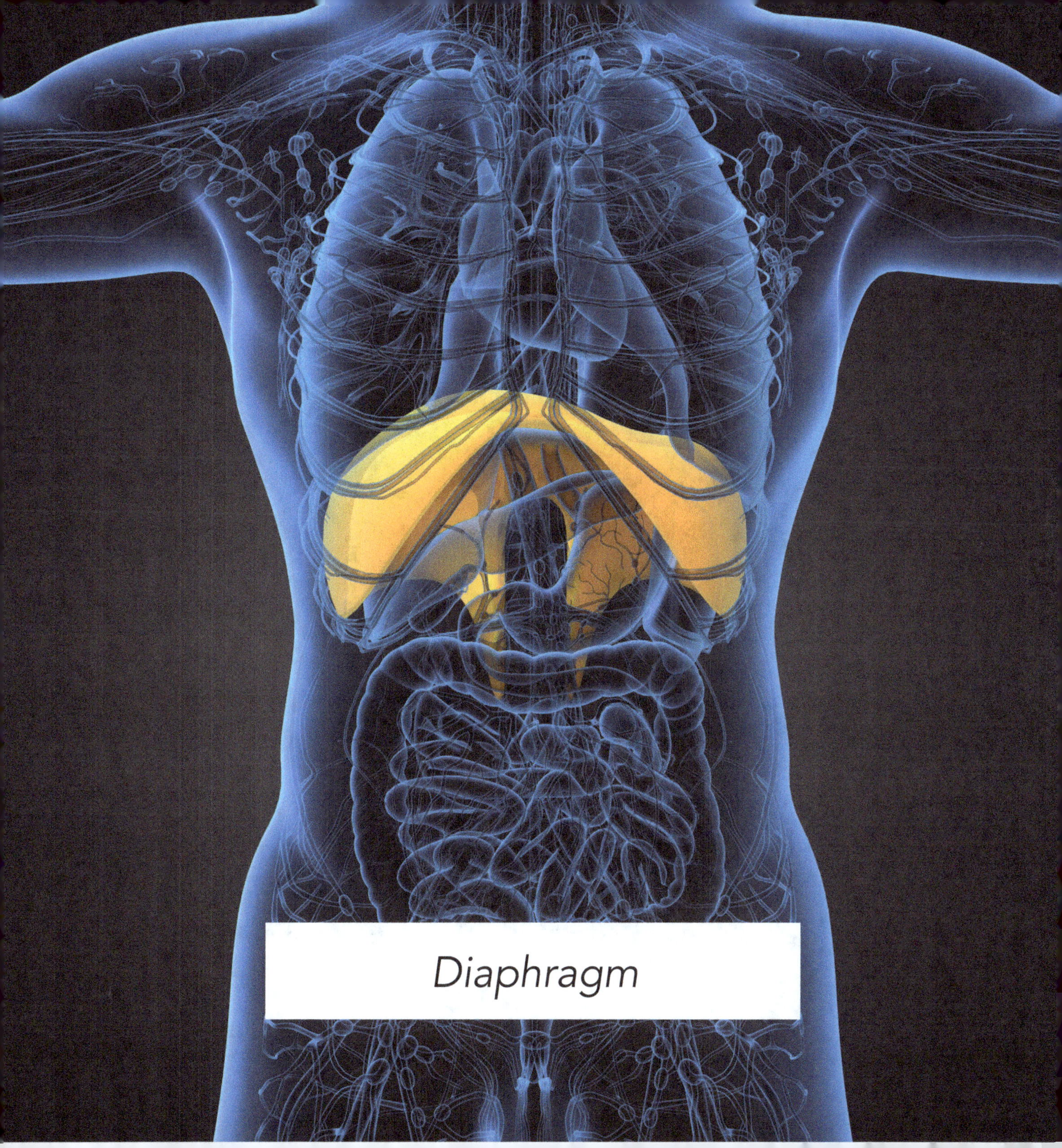
Diaphragm

Inhalation

The lungs are housed inside this pleural cavity. When you inhale or take air in, your diaphragm tightens down or contracts and moves in a downward motion. This increases the space in your pleural cavity and your lungs can expand. The intercostal muscles that are located between your ribs also help you to expand the chest cavity. These motions cause a vacuum effect that helps you suck air into your lungs. This is the process we know as **inhalation.**

Just as your ribs were raised when your diaphragm was contracting, the opposite happens when you exhale. When the muscles in your ribs relax and you're breathing out, your ribcage goes down and your diaphragm relaxes moving upward.

Exhalation

The space on the interior of the pleural cavity gets smaller and air is expelled out of both lungs. This is the process we call exhalation. If you're exercising, you'll notice that your muscles are working hard to rapidly inhale and exhale out of your lungs.

WHAT CONTROLS YOUR RATE OF BREATHING?

There's a special area at the base of your brain that controls the way you breathe. This center in the brain sends signals along your spine and to all the muscles that play a role in breathing.

These brain signals make sure that your breathing muscles and your diaphragm tighten and relax in a regular pattern. Most of the time this happens in an unconscious way, which simply means you don't think about your breathing most of the time.

You can change the rate of your breathing by breathing faster or slower on purpose. Most people who are in good health can hold their breath for up to two minutes. There are some people who have trained themselves to hold their breath for longer periods of time. Emotions can also change your pattern of breathing. If you are scared or angry, it may quicken your pace of breathing.

Holding breath

You'll also need to breathe more often if you're doing a strenuous activity such as exercising. The condition of the air may also cause your breathing to change. Your breathing may slow down if there are irritants in the air.

Sensors located in your airways can give advance warning of irritants in the air. These sensors sometimes cause you to sneeze or cough to get rid of the irritants.

Awesome! Now you know more about the process of how humans breathe. You can find more Biology Books from Baby Professor by searching the website of your favorite book retailer.

Visit
BABY PROFESSOR
EDUCATION KIDS
www.BabyProfessorBooks.com
to download Free Baby Professor eBooks
and view our catalog of new and exciting
Children's Books